Being a Successful Outside Service Provider

A Framework for Success

Gregg Werlein

CONTENTS

ACKNOWLEDGEMENT v

1 INTRODUCTION 1

2 SUCCESS DEFINED 2

3 IMPORTANCE OF A PARTNER RELATIONSHIP 3

4 WHAT CLIENTS WANT.. 4

5 BEING PREPARED 6

6 PROPOSAL DECLINATION... 8

7 PROPOSAL—"HARD COPY"... 10

8 PROPOSAL—"ELECTRONIC COPY"..14

9 PROPOSAL REJECTION 15

10 CAUTION—WORKING WITHOUT A CONTRACT 16

11 CONTRACT 17

12 CAUTION—PROTECTION OF ASSETS 19

13 CAUTION—CONTRACT ADHERENCE 20

14 TRANSITION PREPARATION 22

15 CLIENT SUPPORT DURING TRANSITION 24

16 CAUTION—PERSONNEL CHANGES 26

17 TRANSITION 27

18 CAUTION—PERFORMING SERVICES DURING TRANSITION 30

19 ACCOUNT TEAM TRAINING...31

20 ACCOUNT TEAM SUPPORT 33

21 CAUTION—OUT OF SCOPE WORK.. 34

22   PERFORMANCE OF SERVICES.. 35

23   CAUTION—STAY CONNECTED TO TEAM MEMBERS............................ 39

24   DEDICATED TEAM MEMBERS... 42

25   CAUTION—REPLACING A TEAM MEMBER 43

26   RESELL 45

27   RENEWAL.. 47

28   CLOSING COMMENTS 48

      ABOUT THE AUTHOR.. 49

ACKNOWLEDGEMENTS

I am very grateful to all the individuals that supported and encouraged me while bringing this book to a reality. In particular, I am thankful to Bruce Graham for his insightful suggestions. In addition, I greatly appreciate all of Mike Ryan's contributions, including being my sounding board and proofreader.

1 INTRODUCTION

There is an increasing desire by companies to delegate certain noncore functions to outside service providers as a means of managing their resources and expenses. Companies are realizing:

- Internal resources are not always up-to-date with the latest trends, processes, and procedures.
- Outsourcing is an economically viable alternative to retaining internal resources.
- Service providers' staffing can fluctuate to better handle the typical ebb and flow of work over time by
  - number and duration—the number of resources and their duration can adjust to better match the current level of work;
  - skills—resources can be augmented when specialized skills are required; and
  - location—resources can be realigned to better match location of work.

This growing trend in outsourcing is creating greater competition, resulting in companies placing increasing demands on providers for their services including

- lower cost,
- greater cost savings, and
- increased performance expectations.

Also, companies are exhibiting a lack of loyalty to their existing service providers. They are very willing to move to another provider at the sacrifice of the current one for any number of reasons, even for reasons not related to poor performance.

Being a successful service provider, therefore, is not particularly easy. What follows is a "framework" for becoming more successful in securing and maintaining business. [Note: The term "framework" is intentionally used because a supporting structure of practices is required to achieve lasting success.]

2 SUCCESS DEFINED

"Coming together is a beginning; keeping together is progress; working together is success."
— *Henry Ford*

To know whether you are successful requires an understanding of what success means.

Success is "the accomplishment of an aim or purpose." Therefore, any successful business relationship only occurs when *both* parties feel the relationship is beneficial to them, meeting their goals and objectives.

A successful business relationship, often referred to as a "partner relationship," is where the participants exhibit the following attributes:

- Trust
- Respect
- Openness
- Collaboration

A partner relationship occurs when "you/me" becomes "us." It is a relationship much like a personal relationship, meant to last for an extended period of time. Therefore, each partner remains cognizant of the need to keep the focus on the respect and openness beyond the contract-negotiation phase.

A lasting partner does not just happen; it develops over time. Efforts to build a healthy and strong relationship with a company, therefore, need to begin with the initial contact.

3 IMPORTANCE OF A PARTNER RELATIONSHIP

"We cannot accomplish all that we need to do without working together."
— Bill Richardson

Benefits a service provider may experience in a partner relationship include being more positively viewed than other competing firms and considered a trusted adviser. This positive impression leads to client loyalty, which in turn potentially leads to contract extensions and expansion of services.

Be alert, however, to a client trying to use the "partner relationship" to seek assistance in areas outside of the contract terms. Do not let yourself be taken advantage of in this respect. See section 13, "Caution—Contract Adherence."

Retaining an existing client brings the added benefit of being a lot less costly than seeking a new client.

4 WHAT CLIENTS WANT

"If there is any one secret of success, it lies in the ability to get the other person's point of view and see things from that person's angle as well as your own."
— Henry Ford

While each company is unique, there are similarities among companies in what they seek from an outside service provider. Typical expectations of a provider include the following:

- Demonstrating an interest in working with them

    o Responsiveness
    o Good listener
    o Long-term goal oriented
    o Proactive interaction

        ▪ Cost-saving suggestions
        ▪ Process-improvement suggestions
        ▪ Forewarning of potential issues

- Understanding them, including the following:

    o Values
    o Culture
    o Expectations
    o Processes and procedures

- Having a proven track record

    o Excellent client service
    o Competitive pricing
    o Cost savings
    o Best practices

- Having a good reputation
  - o Reliable
  - o Knowledgeable
  - o Professional
  - o Trustworthy

Successfully securing a service contract with a customer and developing a partner relationship with them largely depends on understanding and then meeting their expectations of you.

5 BEING PREPARED

"Before anything else, preparation is the key to success."
— Alexander Graham Bell

A successful business relationship typically begins in responding to a company's "request for a proposal" (RFP) for providing certain services. Proper preparedness helps ensure the most comprehensive submittal by a more efficient use of time in its preparation.

Common elements, ready beforehand, enhance the effectiveness in preparing a response and should include the following:

- Prepared answers to questions typically asked by potential clients

  Ready answers about such topics as general company information, staffing qualifications, and experience improve preparation efficiency.

- Structure for delivery of services

  Strategies for providing required staffing and how to support them—including their technology—speed up determining the staffing requirements and simplify the preparation process.

- Documented case studies

  Case studies provide assurance to a potential client of your ability to perform the requested services. The best case studies are those that closely reflect the services you are being asked to provide and are relatively recent.

- Available references, including testimonies

  Good references and testimonies provide support regarding your ability to provide the desired services and can help sway a company's decision in your favor.

Being adequately prepared permits a greater focus on company-specific aspects of an RFP, helping to ensure the best possible response.

6 PROPOSAL DECLINATION

"Have the courage to say no. Have the courage to face the truth. Do the right thing because it is right. These are the magic keys to life with integrity."
— *W Clement Stone*

Receipt of an RFP initially requires a decision. Do you present a proposal or not?

A declination is proper for a variety of reasons, including the following:

- Lack of time to adequately respond
- Lack of required resources

Other reasons to decline to respond may revolve around how and why you received the RFP and what your chances of success are. For an example, you may consider the RFP only a formality for negotiating with an incumbent service provider by the company and, therefore, not worth your time and effort in submitting a response.

Declining to respond to an RFP should always afford the possibility of working with the company in the future. Maintain contact with the company on a semiregular basis to keep your name in front of them and to underscore a desire to work with them in the future.

Consider doing the following:

- Include them in newsletter mailings.
- Send them flyers on relevant subjects.
- Maintain personal contact.

    Personal communication (e.g., phone calls, informal meetings) is essential for establishing a positive connection, and therefore, possible future consideration.

Whatever you do to stay in touch with the company, do not stop once you have started. Stopping something you began is likely to cause the company to have a more unfavorable impression of you than doing nothing at all.

As a respected service provider, you are responsible for responding when you can investigate the opportunity properly and create the most compatible solution for both *entities.*

7 PROPOSAL—"HARD COPY"

Responding to an RFP is the first step toward developing a successful relationship with the company, and it needs to be a positive step. First impressions do matter!

Consider the following actions in preparing an RFP response:

- Establish a plan and a timeline for completing the proposal.

  o Avoid waiting until the last minute to finish the submittal.

    The quality and thoroughness of the submittal are likely to suffer if you do.

  o Submit the proposal promptly to underscore your interest—the sooner the better.

- Find out as much as possible about the company, how they operate, and the reason(s) for the RFP to better tailor the proposal.

  Your due diligence should include determining the following:

  o Individual(s) handling the procurement process to assess their knowledge of the requested services

    The interest and focus of procurement people, for example, are typically focused on what the services are going to cost and not the services themselves.

  o Assessment factors for selecting the service provider

    Knowing what is most important to the company helps focus your RFP response appropriately.

  o Extent of the scope of work

    Understanding the magnitude of the work and its complexities is essential in determining staffing and pricing. (Developing a submittal sometimes necessitates making assumptions about the scope of work for various reasons. Documenting those assumptions in the proposal is important to avoid future misunderstandings regarding the extent of work covered by your proposal.)

o   Any requirement for retaining client personnel

A company's requirement that you keep certain employees adds a degree of complexity that requires attention in the preparation of the proposal. One complexity is the need to integrate these employees into your firm while assuming the responsibility for delivering the contractual services. Also, possible personnel issues involving them need to be considered:

- Resentment toward you over the change
- Lack of commitment to your firm
- Lingering performance issues

o   Arrangement for providing team members with their required technology (computers, software, and phones) and support

Having the proper technology and support available for team members is necessary to avoid delays in the commencing of the desired services and inefficiencies in its delivery. Also, there may be cost implications to consider depending on who is providing the technology and the necessary support.

o   Conference calls and reporting requirements

It is important to understand the requirement of participating in calls and reporting, given the potential need for additional resources if the time commitment is excessive, due to team members being less efficient at performing the actual services.

- Include a transition period for assuming the duties of providing the designated services.

  This period is crucial for a smooth handoff of responsibilities between parties. Also, it needs to occur before the specified contractual start date, so the performance of the services commences on time.

  Refer to sections 14 and 17, "Transition Preparation" and "Transition," respectively, for additional information.

- Have a plan for staffing the transition team and afterward, the account team.

  Properly staffed teams performing the right tasks are essential to fulfilling the obligations of the contract and achieving sustainable profitability.

- Address how staffing and finances may vary over time.

  Potential changes to the staffing level due to fluctuation in work over the course of the contract require consideration in the proposal. Also requiring consideration is the typical annual increase in staffing expenses.

- Stress the value you can bring to the client's organization.
    o Show how you can help them succeed.
    o Offer other services you can provide that may be beneficial to them.

- Explain what separates you from your competitors.

  Being able to differentiate yourself from competitors makes your proposal stand out. However, do not make statements that cannot be substantiated or are directed negatively at any competitor. Employing such tactics may result in the company developing an unfavorable impression of you.

- Make the proposal easy to read and understand.

  Provide all requested information clearly and avoid extraneous information. Be concise, and if necessary, refer to sections of the RFP in lieu of restating redundant information and explanations. A third-party review will help to accomplish this.

- Make the submittal professional in appearance and content.

  A good-looking proposal is a good start in making a positive first impression with the company. (Effective use of graphics and images can help with this.)

- Do not overpromise.

  Overpromising your capabilities or making misleading statements can lead to mistrust in you by the company, a major contributor for failing to achieve a long-term relationship with them.

- Do not have a mindset of "let's first win the contract and then figure out how to deliver the services."

  A "win first" mentality often leads to problems later if securing an agreement means proceeding without adequate staffing and compensation.

- Prepare and practice the contents of the proposal, and think of potential answers to questions should you be called upon to present to the company in person.

  An effective presentation may help win acceptance of your proposal over other competitors.

The more you can demonstrate your suitability and compatibility to the company, the greater likelihood they will view your proposal positively.

8 PROPOSAL—"ELECTRONIC COPY"

More and more companies are soliciting proposals through websites. The reasons are varied but include the following:

- Provides consistency in receiving proposal information

  A website dictates how you must respond.

- Makes proposal comparisons easier

  Receipt of information in a consistent manner through a website makes comparing responses simpler.

- Simplifies communications

  Handling all communications through the website provides consistency and record keeping.

Follow the dos and don'ts mentioned in the preceding section to the extent possible, when responding, given the restrictions imposed by the site when responding to a web-based RFP.

9 PROPOSAL REJECTION

"I've learned that mistakes can often be as good a teacher as success."
— Jack Welch

Follow up with the company should your proposal not be accepted. This is important for the following reasons:

- Addresses any misunderstandings regarding your submittal, potentially leading to further consideration now or in the future
- Underscores a desire to work with the company at some future point in time
- Provides an opportunity to establish an ongoing dialog with the company
- Provides the opportunity to learn how to make future proposals better

Following up with the company after the rejection of your proposal can be the first step in marketing yourself to them for future consideration in providing services. (This is also very important when a third-party consultant is involved helping the company with the RFP. They may serve as a conduit for future business opportunities, given their work with other clients.)

10 CAUTION—WORKING WITHOUT A CONTRACT

There might be times when a client desires that services start before the execution of a contract. Reasons for avoiding any such requests include the following:

- Legal issues

  Without an executed contract, the terms and conditions contained within it are unenforceable. Resolving a problem that might arise, therefore, would solely depend on the cooperation and goodwill of the client, a weak position for you regarding the dispute.

- Liability issues

  The absence of an executed contract leaves you, as the service provider, in a weak position relating to liability issues (physical damage, personal damage, and loss of business) that may arise during performing the work.

- Relationship issues

  Performing work with improperly trained staff and a lack of established processes and procedures is likely to result in undesirable issues arising, thereby beginning the relationship with the client in a negative way.

If circumstances require that services must start before the execution of the contract, take steps to protect yourself as much as possible with a document that provides some degree of protection for you in performing the services. Have a standardized form, vetted by your legal department, available for use in such instances, which may be quickly modified for use with a client. Also, always receive some sort of acknowledgment and acceptance from the client to avoid future misunderstandings. (A good client understands this requirement.)

Performing work without a contract is a risky proposition with potentially dire consequences for your firm.

11 CONTRACT

"When one side benefits more than the other that's a win-lose situation. To the winner it might look like success for a while, but in the long run it breeds resentment and distrust."
— Stephen Covey

There are two common pitfalls to avoid during the development of a contract. The first is a lack of understanding regarding full-service outsourcing on the part of the client. This is a different relationship from that with a supplier or vendor that the client is likely to know. This is especially true of clients who are outsourcing services for the first time. Their first draft of a contract, therefore, may lack agreement on key performance categories and the proper language for their measurement.

The second is the choice to use an industry-standard contract. Although it can be quite tailored and specific, it may not reflect either party's best interest.

Consider the following in developing a fair contract:

- Ensure you are willing and able to fulfill all terms and conditions of the contract.

  Overpromising what you can produce/provide leads to negative consequences, particularly the loss of the client's trust.

- Address the following:
  - Provided services
  - Implementation of services
  - Cost of services, including possible future adjustments
  - Staffing, including potential future changes
  - Attainable performance measurements
  - Escalation process for issue resolution
  - Process for transitioning service responsibilities

- o Time allocation for transitioning of service responsibilities
- o Work not covered by the contract
- o Termination provision(s)

- Eliminate vague statements.

  Vague statements often lead to future misunderstandings with the client and loss of revenue.

- Address any assumptions made in the proposal.

  Validate any assumptions before finalizing a contract, given their potential impact on the contract's terms and conditions.

- Do not permit a change in the scope of work during contract negotiations without proper adjustments to the terms and conditions.

Ensure appropriate individuals receive a copy of the contract. It is important that persons responsible for fulfilling the terms and conditions of the contract thoroughly understand them.

If an agreement on terms and conditions is unattainable, do not be afraid to walk away, as achieving success will prove difficult. Also, entering into an unfavorable contract can create a dysfunctional relationship with the client, potentially leading to a negative impression of you in the marketplace.

12 CAUTION—PROTECTION OF ASSETS

The two greatest assets of a service provider are its team members and intellectual property. Therefore, consider protecting these assets when entering into a contract.

- Team members

  A lot of time and money go into making effective team members. Ultimately it is their effectiveness that determines your success with clients and your business. This effectiveness may also lead to a client's desire to pilfer one or more of the team members from you and have them join the client team.

  Consider including a noncompete provision within the contract to prevent a client from approaching team members with a job offer. At a minimum, incorporate contract language forbidding a client from contacting any team member with a job offer without first securing your approval. This is critical since you not only lose a valuable resource, but you also incur all the issues associated with backfilling the position. (It is also fair that this language is mutual.)

- Intellectual property

  A client is likely to expect to retain ongoing rights to use the intellectual property you consider proprietary following the expiration of a contract (e.g., process manuals, forms, databases, electronic portals).

  The contract should plainly state what intellectual property the client may retain following the expiration of the contract and under what conditions, if any.

Failure to include protective language in the contract may lead to the loss of team members and the exclusive use of your intellectual property, thereby lessening the need for your services by the client.

13 CAUTION—CONTRACT ADHERENCE

Adherence to contract provisions is crucial for having a viable contract. Permitting deviation from the contract to occur, without proper documentation, may lead to unintentional changes to the terms and provisions of the contract, including making parts of the contract nonbinding.

For example, performing work not covered by the contract may result in not receiving compensation for the work. In addition, it could create expectations on the part of the client that you will continue to complete such work in the future without changes to staffing and compensation. (Generally, this is called "scope creep.")

Two methods for dealing with contract deviations are contract addendums and letter contracts:

- Addendum

  A deviation that essentially alters any terms or provisions of the contract requires an addendum. It is a legal document used when adding, changing, correcting, or modifying a contract as necessary. Much like the core contract, an addendum requires signatures by authorized individuals of both parties for it to become binding.

- Letter contract

  A letter contract is essentially a simplified contract used when the deviation is an exception to the terms and provisions of the contract. Taking on a special activity from the client, which is not covered by the contract, is an example where the use of a letter contract is appropriate. Such a contract can take many forms, but should specifically outline all relevant aspects of the request and be duly authorized by both parties.

With both methods, be sure work scope, service expectations, term, and a measure of success/failure are clearly stated.

Deviating from the terms and provisions of a contract can have dire consequences unless you are covered by the appropriate documentation.

14 TRANSITION PREPARATION

"Success depends upon preparation, and without such preparation there is sure to be failure."
— Confucius

Be prepared to commence required activities at the beginning of the transition phase to avoid loss of valuable time while getting organized.

Consider the following in your preparation:

- Develop a tentative plan for the following:
    - Identifying the transition steps and their timeline
    - Identifying the information required from the client and timing for receiving it

- Identify a transition team incorporating the following:
    - Executive leadership, responsible for the following:
        - Developing the client relationship
        - Ensuring adherence to the contract terms and conditions
        - Supporting the transition leader
    - Transition leadership, responsible for the following:
        - Supporting the development of a client relationship
        - Ensuring adherence to the contract terms and conditions
        - Interfacing with the client on a day-to-day basis
        - Managing team members
        - Facilitating team training
        - Securing the team's technology
    - Team members with the necessary skills and experience

- Ensure team members' understanding of the following:

  o Relevant contract provisions
  o Expectations of them
  o Processes and procedures
  o Escalating process for issues

- Arrange appropriate support resources to avoid inefficiencies at the commencement of the transition, including the following, if not provided by the client:

  o Standard processes and procedures
  o Standard forms
  o Technology (computers, software, and phones)

In addition to the above-mentioned elements, be prepared to provide the following ancillary personnel support from the following departments:

- Human resources
- Risk management
- Legal
- Subject-matter experts

It is also imperative that the client prepares properly during this phase. Communicate to the client the importance of proper preparation, and set expectations for collaboration. See section 15, "Client Support during Transition."

Proper preparation is essential in accomplishing an effective transition, thus achieving results quickly and noticeably and thereby creating a positive impression with the client.

15 CLIENT SUPPORT DURING TRANSITION

"The way a team plays as a whole determines its success. You may have the greatest bunch of individual stars in the world, but if they don't play together, the club won't be worth a dime."
— Babe Ruth

Client support is essential for the transition to be successful with minimal issues. Without such support the transition team will face significant obstacles, potentially impacting their performance. These obstacles include the following:

- Lack of institutional knowledge of the projects, decision makers, and stakeholders
- Incomplete program and project assignments with insufficient support from client personnel
- Restricted access to electronic systems for the following:
    - Management
    - Reporting
    - Supporting documentation
    - Intranet
    - Accounting and general ledger information
    - Other vendor information

Desired support includes the following:

- Patronage of executives
- Day-to-day leadership
- Adequate resources
- Access to relative information: processes and procedures, reports, contracts, etc.

Work with the client to

- reach agreement on the transition steps and timing,
- understand when and how to share pertinent information,
- introduce each other to team members and the leaders,
- create an alignment matrix for matching partners on the client side for collaboration with your team members,
- ensure transition members and leaders understand their roles and responsibilities,
- ensure transition members know the expectations of them, and
- develop an escalation process for addressing any issue that might arise.

A lack of adequate client support significantly hampers the team's ability for achieving a successful transition.

16 CAUTION—PERSONNEL CHANGES

It is common for clients to have one team involved in the proposal and contract phases (e.g., procurement) and a different team when implementing the transition phase (e.g., accounting, facility management).

With a change in personnel comes potential challenges in working with individuals who have different operating styles, levels of knowledge, and expectations. Complicating the situation is the possibility this change in personnel feeling resentful towards you due to

- fear of losing their jobs,
- fear of losing status and influence,
- fear of changing the status quo, and
- fear of outsourcing being a negative performance statement on them.

Getting to know these individuals and adjusting for their differences is important while entering the transition phase.

17 TRANSITION

"The only way to make sense out of change is to plunge into it, move with it, and join the dance."
— Alan W. Watts

An effective transition establishes the foundation for interacting with the client on a day-to-day basis upon commencement of the stipulated services. It is also a time for solidifying the client's impression of you. You want it to be good.

A successful transition involves the following activities:

- Assembling a transition team

  The transition team is responsible for completing the preparatory work necessary for the permanent team (the account team) to assume the performance of the desired services from the client by the stated date in the contract.

  Having a strong and experienced team is necessary for completing all the preparatory tasks successfully.

- Making preparations

  Proper preparations involve the following:

  o Becoming acquainted with the client's team

    Refer to sections 15 and 16, "Client Support during Transition" and "Caution—Personnel Changes," respectively.

  o Understanding the client's expectations

    It is important there be a shared understanding of expectations, and an escalation process should be in place to address any lingering differences to avoid negativity that may impact the transition.

- o Establishing the processes, procedures, and forms to be used

  This is vital to ensure proper performance by team members at the start of the transition.

- o Securing the necessary technology and security clearances

  A delay in having the required technology and security requirements in place will hamper commencing the transition on time.

- o Becoming knowledgeable about the status of current assignments or projects and new pending ones

  Knowing this information helps in understanding the initial workload, which permits better allocation of the team's resources when providing the desired services begins.

- Onboarding and training account team members

  A transition is not entirely complete until the account team successfully assumes the day-to-day service activities. Therefore, complete the onboarding and training of the account team members before the specified commencement date to ensure a proper handoff from the transition team.

  Refer to section 19, "Account Team Training," for information concerning the training of account team members.

Include the following actions for a successful transition:

- Adhering to the contract provisions

  Failure to follow contract requirements can set a dangerous precedence going forward or result in a breach of contract. Refer to section 21, "Caution—Out-of-Scope Work."

- Meeting regularly with the client

  Holding regular meetings helps ensure the transition stays on track, addresses any misunderstandings, and fosters the development of a healthy relationship.

- Obtaining proper approval for a requested deviation from the contract terms

  Unauthorized deviation from contract terms may lead to unintended consequences: losing revenue, modifying contractual terms, changing the client's expectations, or being unprepared to assume the desired services on time. Refer to section 21, "Caution—Out-of-Scope Work."

Experience shows that successful transitions also provide communication to at least two levels. The first is communication to the teams and personnel affected by the transition itself as well as the post-transition business environment. And the second communication is to the broader business, which should include the driver or reason for the change and the expected goals driven by the change itself (e.g., better customer service, lower costs, speed to market). These communications can include one or more of the following:

- Newsletters
- Blog updates
- Transition home page or company portal

Do not underestimate the importance of a successful transition in demonstrating your capabilities to the client and building acceptance with them.

18 CAUTION—PERFORMING SERVICES DURING TRANSITION

The transition period is intended to prepare the account team members to assume the responsibility for providing the desired services. However, a client might ask you to commence performing services before the conclusion of the transition period. Resist such requests. Undertaking the performance of services during the transition period takes the focus away from completing the preparation tasks and may lead to performance issues due to the following reasons:

- Transition team members being ill-prepared to perform the services for lack of appropriate training on processes and procedures
- Additional stress placed on transition team members resulting from the added responsibilities
- Account team not suitably prepared to provide desired services by stated commencement date within the contract

Insist on adding staff to the team if it is necessary to start performing the services during the transition period in order to ensure the transition activities are completed properly. Also, set the correct expectations with the client for beginning the services early, since the processes and procedures may or may not be in place and for the lack of training of the team members relative to those processes and procedures.

Make sure any such activities are covered by the appropriate documentation. Refer to section 13, "Caution—Contract Adherence."

19 ACCOUNT TEAM TRAINING

"It's all to do with training; you can do a lot if you're properly trained."
— *Elizabeth II*

The transition team is to complete training of the account team before the contractual commencement start date, including the following:

- Contract provisions

  Account team members need to know their contractual obligations to perform appropriately and the process for assessing their performance.

- Processes and procedures

  Account team members need to know the processes and procedures they are to follow in delivering the designated services beginning on the start date.

- The organizational structure of the client

  Account team members need to know the roles and responsibilities of the individuals within the client's organizational structure to interact with them appropriately while delivering the designated services. Also, it is critical that team members know who the decision maker(s) are to avoid taking direction inappropriately from someone else.

- Escalation structure

  Account team members need to understand what issues to escalate and how to do so when appropriate.

- Support structure

  Account team members need to know how to obtain support for company and client matters.

- Acquired client personnel training, if applicable

  Retaining former client personnel requires assimilating them into your company's culture and helping them become knowledgeable about your practices. Also, there may be some lingering hard feelings on their part about having been let go by their company as well as a reluctance toward any changes to the processes and procedures they are familiar with. Therefore, it is necessary to develop plans to make them feel wanted and to get them integrated into the team.

In addition, the transition team must ensure the account team members are appropriately equipped (e.g., computers, phones) to perform the contractual services and possess the required accesses (e.g., databases, security).

Properly trained and equipped account team members are essential if they are to successfully deliver the desired services and build a lasting relationship with the client.

20 ACCOUNT TEAM SUPPORT

"Unity is strength...when there is teamwork and collaboration, wonderful things can be achieved."
— Mattie Stepanek

Continued adherence to the processes and procedures developed during the transition is one of the hardest behavioral components to maintain. Therefore, continued involvement of transition team members for a period of time helps ensure a smooth handoff of responsibilities and continued adherence to the established processes and procedures. Consider frequent touch-points during the first one or two-quarters to help achieve a successful transition.

Maintaining the availability of the transition team enables them to assist the account team with questions and issues arising during the early stages of providing the designated services, thus helping to ensure their performance is positive and productive.

21 CAUTION—OUT-OF-SCOPE WORK

Out-of-scope work is work either not specifically covered by the contract or outside of the established processes and procedures. Authorized approval is necessary before undertaking such work to avoid the following issues:

- A breach of contract
- Increased legal liability
- Additional expenses
- Misunderstandings
- Changing client expectations

The client may expect you to expand your level of services without any adjustment to compensation by performing such work.

Refer to section 13, "Caution—Contract Adherence."

Any approval received for deviating from the established processes and procedures or contract terms and conditions is to be documented for possible reference, should any questions arise later concerning the deviation.

22 PERFORMANCE OF SERVICES

"Desire is the key to motivation, but it's the determination and commitment to an unrelenting pursuit of your goal – a commitment to excellence – that will enable you to attain the success you seek."
— Mario Andretti

It is highly unlikely that a partner relationship will develop with the client unless the account team delivers the contracted services as expected, if not better than anticipated. Therefore, the account team's performance is to include the following:

- Adhering to contract's terms and conditions

    o Meeting contract obligations
    o Avoiding deviation from contract obligations without appropriate approval

- Following established processes and procedures and obtaining proper approval before permitting any deviation from them

    o Ensuring proper delivery of services
    o Ensuring the right parties make required decisions

- Keeping meetings and conference calls to a minimum

    Attending meetings and conference calls take time, and a negative impact on the team's efficiency occurs when they are excessive.

- Keeping reports to a minimum and as simple as possible

    Preparing reports take time and more so when they are complex. Therefore, weigh the value of creating a given report against its potential adverse impact on the team's efficiency in the delivery of services.

- Tracking and documenting performance

  o Knowing what didn't go well leads to process improvement.
  o Knowing what went well counters client's focus on undesirable situations.
  o Knowing what went well contributes to achieving a high-performance team.

- Understanding that "the client is not always right, but they are the client"

  It is important for team members to know there will be times the client disagrees with their professional opinion on an issue. The client is not necessarily right, but they are the client and have the final decision. However, such a decision by the client must be documented. The documentation alleviates a possible problematic situation if there is a question about the decision in the future.

- Employing the escalation process when appropriate

  Escalation of significant issues is critical to ensure compliance with the terms and conditions of the contract as well as the agreed to processes and procedures. Failure to do so may lead to a conflict with the client and

  o negative performance,
  o unwanted liability,
  o loss of revenue, and
  o unknowingly modifying the terms and conditions of the contract.

- Seeking improvement opportunities

  Identifying and then implementing improvements is critical in achieving long-term success with the client for the following reasons:

  o Demonstrates your commitment to seeing the client succeed
  o Demonstrates the added value you bring to the client
  o Distinguishes you from your competitors

- Holding and documenting regular account team meetings

  Account team meetings should be a forum to help promote team building and for the following purposes:

  o Sharing ideas and concerns

    An open forum lets team members know that their thoughts and concerns are important, thus preventing a buildup of frustration on their part.

  o Sharing pertinent information pertaining to the client and your company

    - Keeping team members informed of what is happening with the account from both the client's and the company's perspectives contributes significantly to harmony in the team. Dealing with unknowns typically creates discomfort for individuals.
    - Knowing what is occurring with your business outside of just their account makes them feel part of a larger organization and reduces the feeling of isolation.

    Sharing information builds trust and counteracts false information and rumors. Informed employees are more contented employees.

- o Acknowledging achievements

  Discussing successes and good performance are positive motivators for team members.

- Keeping internal matters internal

  Sharing internal information with the client inappropriately is likely to create issues for the company and may have an adverse impact on your relationship with the client.

Strive to exceed expectations in the delivery of your services to help strengthen the bond with the client.

23 Caution—Stay Connected to Team Members

"True leadership lies in guiding others to success. In ensuring that everyone is performing at their best, doing the work they are pledged to do and doing it well."
— *William Pollard*

Sustaining success requires a high level of performance by the account team. It is not unusual, however, for attention to the account team to be diverted by management to other business priorities over time. A lack of attention may lead to a feeling of alienation among team members, causing frustration, dissatisfaction, and low morale and thus impacting their performance.

Staying connected to team members is important for the following reasons:

- Counteracts a sense of abandonment due to a lack of the following:
  - Training
  - Mentoring
  - Resources
  - Appreciation

- Counteracts negativity buildup

  Team members are more likely to make disparaging comments to the client about the company as their frustration and dissatisfaction increase over what they deem to be inappropriate support. This is particularly true if they believe there is a negative impact on their performance due to the perceived lack of support.

- Counteracts shifting of loyalties

  Team members may shift their loyalties from the company to the client as their frustration and dissatisfaction grow over time. This change in loyalties may manifest itself in various ways, including

  o routinely taking on work not covered by the contract just because the client asked them;
  o regularly taking the client's side on issues, even to the company's detriment;
  o ever-increasing focus on the client's needs/desires over those of the company's; and
  o not being supportive of company initiatives.

- Counteracts desire to seek other employment

  Team members residing at a client's place of business or elsewhere are more susceptible to feelings of separation as "connection" with the company is more tenuous and, therefore, are more likely to seek employment elsewhere.

Making sure that team members know and feel part of a larger organization that is supporting them is important in avoiding them feeling disconnected. Also, it is important to develop a rapport with team members on an individual basis. A person likes to know that his or her efforts are appreciated.

Consider the following for staying connected with team members:

- Foster two-way dialog

  Team members want to know you are interested in what they have to say.

- Fulfill commitments

  Not keeping your commitments erodes trust.

- Hold regular check-in meetings/calls for the following reasons:

  o Discuss what is occurring elsewhere, within the company and industry.
  o Discuss the account: client feedback, issues, and support.
  o Present development topics.

- Hold semiannual one-on-one sessions, preferably face-to-face, for the following reasons:

  o Discuss personal goals and objectives.
  o Discuss performance, with an emphasis on positives.
  o Discuss any personal concerns/issues.
  o Discuss development and growth opportunities.

These sessions are to be documented for future reference.

Success requires a team of dedicated and motivated individuals. Staying connected with team members is paramount in achieving the desired level of dedication and motivation from them.

24 DEDICATED TEAM MEMBERS

"Talent wins games, but teamwork and intelligence wins championships."
— *Michael Jordan*

Dedicated team members are essential for having a high-performing team, which is critical to developing and maintaining a good relationship with a client.

A split focus occurs with non-dedicated team members when they are involved with multiple assignments, potentially hurting the team's chemistry and performance.

Providing the client with the highest level of professional performance possible requires committed team members.

25 Caution—Replacing a Team Member

Provide as much notice as possible to the client when it becomes necessary for you to replace a team member. An unfavorable client reaction is likely with a last-minute change to the team. The notice is also a helpful tool to seek the client's buy-in for the change.

Points to consider when notifying the client to include the following:

- Reason(s) for the change
- Transition plan for replacing the team member
- Schedule for completing the transition

It is best the notice is given in person or via a phone call, followed up with appropriate documentation to the client. It is also preferable that the notice is provided by the executive leader to underscore your commitment to the relationship.

Stay in touch with the client throughout the process to keep them updated on the progress of the transition and to address any of their concerns. This will help to assure the client that your level of service is not going to suffer during or after the change.

Include the following in response to a client's request to replace a team member:

- Reason(s) for the request:
    - Knowing the reason(s) may afford the opportunity to suggest an alternative to the removal of a team member and the issues involved in doing so.
    - Knowing the reason(s) allows for steps to be taken to avoid a similar request in the future.

- Requirement for a transition period

    Finding a replacement team member and completing the training of the person requires time.

Close interaction with the client is indispensable in replacing a team member to assure a common understanding, to manage expectations, and to obtain their cooperation.

26 RESELL

"Learning and innovation go hand in hand. The arrogance of success is to think that what you did yesterday will be sufficient for tomorrow."
— *William Pollard*

The key element to achieving a long-term relationship is the reselling of yourself to the client. Reselling is the process of bringing to the client's attention your service value routinely and should begin soon after the contract is signed. However, the actual timing is predicated upon the characteristics of the client.

Your reselling efforts should involve the following:

- Keep your senior management involved.

  Continued top management involvement is a sign of the client's importance to the company, and the desire to forge a long-term partnership with them.

  The interaction needs to be more than just sitting in on a meeting every three or six months. Being passive will not generate the desired reaction from the client. Interact with the client with frequent communications and one-on-one meetings.

- Highlight successes achieved on behalf of the client.

  Unfortunately, clients seem to have a short memory as it relates to the success that you have made on their behalf; therefore, they need to be reminded routinely.

- Highlight lessons learned from a problem and the action taken concerning it.

  Problems will invariably occur during any relationship, requiring the handling of the same in a direct manner. Doing so involves acknowledging a problem, learning about the cause of the problem, and implementing steps to avoid repeating it.

Effectively dealing with a problem may have a longer-lasting positive impact on a client than if the problem had never occurred.

- Highlight how you are adding value.

  Just doing a good job does not guarantee that the client will renew the contract. Often a client thinks that there are others in the marketplace who can do just as good a job as you. Therefore, it becomes important to exhibit your additional value to them—doing something faster, better, and less costly than expected.

  Bringing ideas and suggestions to the client is beneficial regardless of whether the ideas are accepted or not. It demonstrates a commitment to them and their success.

Reselling enhances the probability of extending your contract with the client for the following reasons:

- Counteracts the "what have you done for me today" syndrome clients sometimes exhibit
- Reflects your efforts to see the client succeed
- Helps build client loyalty

Reselling is how you show the client that you are committed to a long-term relationship with them and their success, both now and in the future.

27 RENEWAL

"No one ever attains very eminent success by simply doing what is required of him; it is the amount and excellence of what is over and above the required that determines the greatness of ultimate distinction."
— *Charles Kendall Adams*

Renewals come with two primary challenges from a client:

1. Other companies can perform the same services for perhaps less money.

   Just performing at an expected level tends to lead a client to believe they can receive the same degree of service from others at a potentially reduced cost.

2. The client wants to pay less for more services.

   Companies often request, and expect, a reduction in your cost of services, regardless of your level of performance. Also, they may seek additional services from you at no extra charge.

Overcoming these challenges underscores the importance of reselling yourself throughout the contract term. Refer to section 26, "Resell."

When responding to an RFP for a contract renewal, apply relevant aspects mentioned in section 7, "Proposal—Hard Copy."

Similar to the initial contract, the renewal needs to work for both parties. Refer to section 11, "Contract."

Closely aligned with the ability to secure a renewal is your effectiveness in demonstrating your ability to help the client to be successful and that you have a good working relationship with them.

28 Closing Comments

"The price of success is hard work, dedication to the job at hand, and the determination that whether we win or lose, we have applied the best of ourselves to the task at hand."
— *Vince Lombardi*

There are no expectations that the "framework" for being a more successful service provider offers you any great revelations. But overlooking the elements that make up the "framework" may negatively impact your ability to build the desired partner-type relationship with a client. Without such a relationship, you are just one of many suppliers in the eyes of the client, easily replaced with someone else if they become dissatisfied with your service for any reason.

I wholeheartedly recommend employing the presented practices to create **a framework for success** in your pursuit and retainage of clients.

"Success is neither magical nor mysterious. Success is the natural consequence of consistently applying basic fundamentals."
— *Jim Rohn*

ABOUT THE AUTHOR

Gregg Werlein worked in the corporate world for over forty years as both a client of outsourced services and then eventually as a successfully outsourced service provider himself. In each situation, Gregg led successful teams that included members from both the client and the service provider, working together to meet and exceed the annual and long-term goals. Initially, he worked with an industry-leading corporation employing and directing a variety of service providers on projects throughout the United States. Later, he worked for a Fortune 100 company providing outsourced services to multiple national companies.

In addition, Gregg served as a leader in a number of transitions that included the ownership and responsibility for the relationship and the newly developed process, identification of duties, key performance measurements, and client business reviews. Finally, before retirement, Gregg worked to revive and refresh accounts having service-relationship issues. The successful results were attributed to his excellent organizational skill, leadership, fair and accountable task management, time management, and ability to improve cooperation between the account and client teams.

During his employment, Gregg held a license in architecture, LEED accreditation, and two real-estate broker licenses.

www.ingramcontent.com/pod-product-compliance
Lightning Source LLC
Chambersburg PA
CBHW061223180526
45170CB00003B/1125